A CALL TO REMEMBER

A journey with the Swiss

by

Bernadith Bueno De La Cruz

Edited by Marie Ezekiel
Designed by Tess Ritumalta

ISBN:
Hardbound-978-621-470-121-6
Mobile/Kindle-978-621-470-122-3
Softbound/Paperback-978-621-470-123-0

Published by:
Poetry Planet Book Publishing House
Rosario, Pozorrubio, Pangasinan, Philippines
Contact No.: 09554960044
Email: maritesritumalta@gmail.com

DEDICATION

This book is dedicated to all. To serve as an inspiration to acquire positivity despite of all negativities that surrounds us.

ACKNOWLEDGEMENTS:

My sincere gratitude to Poetry Planet Publishing House for allowing me to publish my written pieces.
As an advocate of preserving humanity, I am humbly commending my parents to this work, by raising me up a strong and open minded person. To my whole family. To my friends who witnessed my struggles and pains, my perseverance and strong will. To my very generous and caring employers who supported me, Monsieur Mathias Ogier and Madame Adrianne Ogier, all the way to make this happen and for treating me as family. To Richard Bryant Jr. who never stop pushing me up to develop myself to live life to the fullest and to be the best version of me, supporting me in all aspects of life.

Thank you all so much!

God bless us all!

INTRODUCTION

Positivity, peace, love and humanity. These are the key points I want to instill into the minds of the readers of this book. As a young age, I grew up answering the call of God, to share my purpose in life to others. In this book is the product of what I've been through in this life, my point of views, and my answer to God's call to spread the Gospel, to share love, to preserve humanity and to live with peace.

PREFACE

"Positive thinking is the key to happiness and contentment." This confirmed the author's conviction, as seen in her book "**A Call to Remember**". Bernadith B. De la Cruz' book is a collection of her thoughts, and it reflects her positive outlook on life. Her devotion to God brought her joy and served as a source of inspiration as she battled homesickness after being separated from her family for far too long. She is currently working in a foreign land to support her family's needs. In the subtitle: "A journey with the Swiss"; her writings were composed while she works for a Swiss family. It also inspired her employer's 8 year old daughter to write poems and be included in this book.

Her love for God, especially when the pandemic struck the world, helped her overcome the terrifying and stressful situations she was forced to face. It is her hope that her fervent emotions, scribbled in forms of poetry, will also help readers who are experiencing bouts of depression and loneliness.

This poetry collection explores the highest levels of emotions such as hope, positivity, and exaltation of God's divine power. It is an antidote that can help cure loneliness and depression. It has the potential to help the reader heal emotionally. A person suffering from loneliness can be helped by nothing more than the kind and comforting words of someone who has experienced the same fate.

It is unquestionably a must-read for all in order to elevate the readers' sense of self-worth, re-establish positivity, and achieve the contentment and tranquility that the author has experienced. These are the motivations behind the creation of this book.

The Publisher

TABLE OF CONTENTS

GIFTED WITH COURAGE

Strength in the face of pain or grief
Have conviction to everyone's belief
From downfall, never loses hope
From failure, never quits, always cope

Courageous people have self-confidence
They found their courage in divine providence
In the midst of difficulties and turmoil
Standing still and strong, nothing and no one can
spoil

They shed a tear but wipe it clear
They mourn, it's true! but not for a year
From turbulence, they are not shaken
Solid foundation of strength, for them, can't be stolen

In times of conflict and confusion
They keep calm, never in haste for conclusion
Always having that positive mindset
Weighing over things that gives a threat

The gift of courage from heaven above
Showered upon all of us through God's love
For God's courage is unfathomable
Given to us by example and it's charitable

STAIRWAY TO HEAVEN

Sparkly and enchanted it seem
To get there, is everyday I dream
In the Scripture, told, no famine in there
All were clothed with purity, in harmony together

Reaching heaven, no more pain
Love and happiness pours like rain
Joy overflows, I can't wait to be there
And live with God, I pray, and be with Him forever

Stairway to heaven, elegant and wonderful
Rich in glory shines through the soul
Full of kindness, lined with fruits of the Holy Spirit
The moment you'll step on it, you will never regret

Blessed are those who remain humble
Keeping the faith even sometimes can't avoid to stumble
Stairway to heaven, magnificent and holy
God is preparing it for us, so seek Him fully

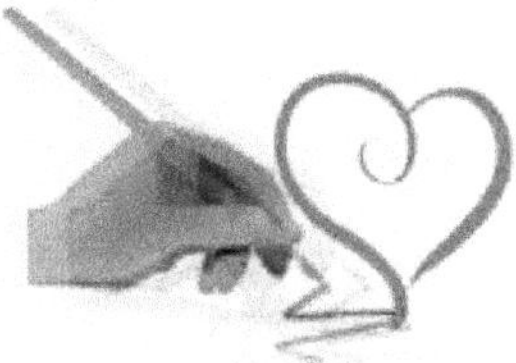

GOD IS MY ROCK

G- od Almighty! My rock, my saviour
O- mnipotent and benevolent, creator
D- eity, all knowing, You oh Lord!

I- ndeed, without You, I am nothing
S- inner I am but by Your precious blood, You've saved me

M- yself is not worthy, but from sin You've forgive me
Y- our love is pure and unconditional, You alone can give

R- ock of my salvation, rescuer of my soul, my shield
O- wner of heaven and earth, all praise to Him
C- reator of the universe, I trust and believe Him
K- ind, loving and merciful, I accepted Him as my personal Lord and Saviour

STRIVING FOR SURVIVAL

In a world full of suffering, I'm a bit lonely
Nothing to be with, no one is available, everyone is
busy

Leaving behind, in darkness and roughness
Feeling suppressed, struggling from uneasiness

From being alone, I work hard, I learned to strive
Nothing, no one to lean on, so I created my own hive

In my hive, my secret abode, I used to climb
Climbing out, I started to grow with time

Strong foundation built, I gain control
I trust my guts, I survived, knowledge from the Scroll

Look at me now! Full bloomed, renewed and God
found
Survivor, brave and strong, yet feet stays on the
ground

LET US SPREAD LOVE

L- iving with love is living life happily
E- ternal blessing from our God Almighty
T- reasure kept in our hearts

U- nderstanding that never departs
S- adness are gone, all vanished

S- ecured from longing love, never felt anguished
P- roud to share and spread love unconditionally
R- acing to give peace, this act is a gift, given us perfectly
E- quality also shows love
A- doration from the Giver above
D- iety, God Himself is the pure love

L- oneliness flee, from once a broken soul
O- rder and peace, now all are in control
V- iolence gone because love suppressed it
E- vil destruction defeated by God's love, the ultimate gift

MOMENTS OF TIME

M- oments of time, so precious as gold
O- rdinary days that sometimes untold
M- emories that never becomes old
E- mbedded into the heart, ain't getting cold
N- othing can stop the time, it is uncontrolled
T- he past is already past, we can't hold
S- haring it to the future, the lessons unfold

O- rchard of experiences that graciously mold
F- laccid personalities that saddens the world

T- ime wasted are already sold
I- t passes by, gone and consequences can't be consoled
M- oments of time, if wasted, you're gonna get sold
E- ither waste or use it with great purpose, chose the latter, be bold!

WHY

Why?
Why instead of doing good,
        people choose evil?
Why instead of generosity,
        majority chooses corruption?

Why?
Why we are fond of destruction?
        destroy our mother earth?
Destroy love, peace and humanity,
        destroy ourselves?

Why?
Why we are so heartless?
        so heartless to kill
To kill the lives, lives that
        struggling to survive?

Why?
Why instead of honesty, we lie?
        people choose to contradict the good
Living in a way that the evil told?
        we forget God!

Why?
Why the balance of the world gone?
        negative won the place
Evil deeds occupied our system
        positive rested behind

Why?
Why are all these happening?
        when are we going to act?
When are we going to lead and voice out?

when are we going to preserve the world
with love, peace and humanity?

The answer lies on you my friend
Yes! within you.

BE AN INSPIRATION

B- e a hope for someone who struggle
E- xpand our hand to those in trouble

A- llow yourself to be the light
N- od our head to God, this is right

I- nspire others with positivity
N- ever cling to negativity
S- hine! carrying the torch of love
P- lanted to us by our God above
I- ndeed nowadays, a lot suffer
R- acing for survival because life is tougher
A- nd maybe one of us can change the situation
T- hrough giving them a powerful inspiration
I- n this world full of difficulties
O- ur love, faith and genuine kindness
N- ext to spreading humanity, are the key to inspire
others

FROM DUST TO DUST

Aphar a Hebrew word for dust
Dust that also refers to earth
God formed man from a dust
Do you agree that we came from dirt?

I do believe in God and Christianity
Without God we are nothing
Humans nowadays lived in immortality
We are all sinners, yet majority are still loving

From dust to dust, a saying goes
So while we live, choose to do good
It's hard but learn to reconcile with your foes
This is a rule that only a few understood

I am not advertising Christianity
I do respect each one's belief
But I can't hide my true identity
Loving God brings me relief

All the earth's riches and goodness
All the knowledge that human got
Turned nothing if people live in stubbornness
We will die, turn to dust, but people forgot

As long as we live
Please do remember, from dust we came
And I strongly believe
To earth we return and dust we become

BEYOND WRECKED

Ambitious you are
You let go from the hands of the Lord
You followed your selfish desires
You followed your envious heart!

Greedy you are
You let go from the will of the Lord
You took what is not yours
You ruined someone's happiness

Killer you are
You let go from the unconditional love of the Lord
Smashed someone's life
You let the bereaved family all in deep sorrow

Back fighter, gossiper you are
You let go from the humbleness of the Lord
You stabbed your neighbors back with false rumors
Leaving them bad into the perception of others

Covetous you are
You let go from the Holy Bond of the Lord
Why you covet your neighbor's husband and wife?
Why you preferred the spirit of lust?

Selfish, user you are
You let go from the kindness of the Lord
You only think of yourself
Using others for your own benefit

Perfectionist you are
You let go from the great mercy of the Lord
You are fast to punish those who wronged you
And don't look at yourself as a sinner too?

People who are choosing an evil deed
As we are all have our freedom to choose
Are all wrecked, beyond wrecked
For they fought against the Lord

Please do remember the golden rule
So we will live happy and don't fall
Fall into the pit of burning fire
And forever suffer and no one in there to inquire

LIVE HAPPY

Living a peaceful life is all that matter
Independently strong and loving, avoid the hater
Violence is a no, choose love and unity instead
Especially when you're at the middle of a living dead

Happy memories are kept, sealed with a kiss
Allow anyone in your circle to be loved and be
blessed
Praying always for the good in this life
Powerful prayers that blocks the unseen dangers
Yearning for happiness, live happy and share it to
others.

NOTHING IMPOSSIBLE

Never stop believing in yourself
One step at a time will make progress
Trust your own instinct, don't hesitate
Humbly bow down in God's presence
Inner self of kindness will push you up
Nothing is impossible to a man who works hard
Genuinely striving with courage and determination

Inside the belief of the impossible, all is surely
possible
Morning and night, you can work for it, you are able
Pressures, just ignore, think of a better solution
Organize each step towards your goal, mind the
caution
Solutions are many, nothing is impossible, go on
Save your energy, stand up from frustration
Indeed, you are courageous, unstoppable
Bestowed upon you, courage, you are undoubtedly
capable
Loving your goal, doing it with passion
Emblem of your success, in the middle of the
impossible, is your great dedication

MINDSET MATTERS

It is a matter of mindset, I may say
Think positively, ignore the hearsay
When you set your mind to succeed
Stick to it, don't be shaken, forsake the greed
Work hard for it with a humble heart

Our mind is a potting tray
We planted it dreams and we pray
Working for it with different speed
Depends on what each and everyone's urgent need
Dedication, courage and strong determination will do
its part

KEEP ON MOVING

Remember in the midst of a weak and ugly situation
After that, rose a strong and beautiful foundation
That once you're a dumb, now you're knowledgeable
In handling mindset of negativity, now in positivity
you're able

Continue to rise from your fall
Dream big and ignore those small
Time flies so fast and yet you're too slow
So keep on moving upwards but feet keep their
below

HOLD ON

Hold on! Hold on! when you feel alone
When you're at the midst of difficulties
When you feel the world abandoned you
And no one in sight to help you, hold on!

Hold on! Hold on! Hang in there my fellow
Struggles will not last forever
Don't ever give up to win the race
Pray! God hear you, hold on!

Hold on! Hold on! After the trials is victory
Don't waste your time crying
Twist the bad situations into positive thinking
You can do it, yes you can! Hold on!

Hold on! Hold on! I know the test of life is not that
easy
But believe in yourself
Be strong and courageous
At the end of the rainbow, there's a pot of gold. Hold
on!

Hold on! Hold on! God will come to rescue you
Bless you abundantly and unexpectedly
If you continue to fight the good fight
You will commit success in due time, hold on!

Hold on! Hold on! My brothers and sisters
Meditate and give yourself a break
Relax, smile and pursue your dreams, whatever it
takes
God loves you dearly, will never forsake you. Hold on!

Hold on! Hold on!
There is HOPE!

ONE DAY IT WILL CHANGE

One day all your cares will be settled
Your tears will dry up
Your fears will become strength
You will become unbeatable, one day!

One day all your sorrows will become happiness
Don't give up continue pursuing your dreams
The test of life will make you strong
You will see your success, one day!

One day you will become prosperous
If your mindset is positive
If you nourish your body and mind to be healthy
You will become unstoppable, one day!

One day you will roar like a lion
You will be the best version of yourself
You will be shocked with the result of your hard work
It will be unbelievable but you'll make it possible, one
day!

One day your battle will be over
All your struggles will just vanish
You will learn a lot from your life experiences
So prepare to celebrate your triumph, one day!

One day God will answer all your prayers
Will cover you with all the protection you needed
Will give you all the love and strength
And so also prepare yourself to spread back the love
to people, one day!

LIFE JOURNEY

In our life, there's a time for everything
Unexpectedly something will happen
Don't ever give up, continue fighting

Daily experiences teach us to sharpen
Our strengths, weaknesses even our mindset
Stand our ground firmly, vigilantly hearken

Being so courageous is a great asset
Unbelievably undeniable gift
Having all of these, granted no more defeat

Silently crying, mourning, happiness theft
It's normal psychologically fine
Tested and proven by time, no tears left

Sorrows come, successful days are in line
Lifestyles turning humans well or unhealthy
Consequences of our choices tastes like wine

It's up to us to write our own story
Wrestle, strive to surpass well this life's journey.

TO MY FRIEND

To my friend who is weary
Trust the Lord and hand it over to Him all your
worries
You will feel His embrace and love
God will catch you and will comfort you

To my friend who has a problem with money today
Strive hard and earn while you can
While you still have the strength to work
Save today so you can have an easy life tomorrow

To my friend who is suffering from a relationship
Learn to walk away and move on if it's toxic and
hurting
Love others but don't forget to love yourself first
As they said, too much love will kill you

To my friend who is physically ill
Please take care of yourself while still you can
We ourselves are accountable of what our health had
gone
But now all I can say is get well soon.

FREEDOM

We are in a cage of horror
Suppressed and in great terror
Pizzazz has been hidden
Hidden by a jealous in power
In the cocoon of purity, we are in safety
Molding our spirit and grow discreetly
And in due time, we'll spread our wings, like a
butterfly, flew beautifully and free.

Treated slave in a foreign land
Discriminated and slapped by an evil hand
Masters that pretending to be royals
Migrant workers still, are being patient and loyal
Sacrifices cannot be measured
Leaving the homeland to earn a living
Why masters are so cruel? Migrant workers are
human!

HOMELESS

Out in the dark
full of pain
eaten by tremendous depression
a huge space of longingness
You are there!
You are there,
sitting with your best friend
the only one
who understands,
who won't leave you
no matter what.
As you are the master
truly loved and cared.
A man's best friend
who felt your deepest emotions.
I, I was there
staring at you
and my heart,
my heart is crying a river
my soul floats into the air
out of nowhere.
Looking at you
is the saddest thing,
I felt in my entire life!
You stared at me back
with a gesture of weakness
your eyes are telling me
all the sorrows
you are now having
but at the corner of your eyes
You are also saying
"don't worry I'm fine"
What a brave soul you are!
Someday,

someday, you will have
whatever you wished for.
and the next time we met,
I predict
You're not homeless anymore
You will be happy
in a home
with your best friend!

STANDING STILL

I am a tree
Standing tall and free
And with all the seasons of life, I'm standing still
I'm strongly rooted, no one can kill

In the summer of my life, I am in great delight
Happiness shines through and spreads light
My leaves all blooms, green and healthy
Because this is all from my positivity

Even in the autumn, all my leaves will fall
Dreams, goals, plans, swayed by the wind, I felt small
I still remain standing, I am fixed, I don't bargain
Knowing that after my fall, there's lesson and I can
start again

In the rainy and winter days, full of sorrow
Heartbreaks remains frozen, in my heart it grow
But I am a tree, strong and rooted
I go out to the rain and snow, feeling it, barefooted

I am a tree
I am strong, I am rooted, I am free
I bear fruit of strength and knowledge of positivity
I'm sharing you all my fruits, pick it, enjoy it, thank
God for this gift of genuinity

DILEMMA

It was in a mind of chaos
In a situation that is hard to choose
They don't know what to do
They don't know where to go

There's a lot of laid choices
Brings stress and silence, shut their voices
Creates a great confusion
And leads to a huge destruction

Dilemma, why oh why you existed?
Consequences of made decisions, untwisted
It causes sometimes mental stress
And puts all aspects of life in a mess

Do you know of someone in this situation?
From the past and to the present generation?
Did you mind giving them a helping hand?
Listening to them and try to understand?

Or are we become so judgemental?
To those suffering from a dilemma who become
sentimental?
Believe me or not, I can tell you truly
We ignored them, don't mind them, fully

A problem that simply we can solve
if love, we choose to spread and be involve
What a wonderful world of brotherhood
That God will bless, yes! Him as our father, would.

ON THE WHEELS

Tough man I know
Through the heat
Through the rain
He is present, always present
Along the road
On the wheels
To earn a living.
A father, a helper
A laborer, but most of all
A hero to his children.
An example to the society
Through his calloused hands
And to now turning charcoal skin
He faces the scorching heat
  of the burning sun
To feed the rumbling stomach
  of anyone in his humble abode
Did you know? I will tell you!
Sometimes he didn't have
  even a single piece of bread
  to satisfy his own starve
He is not thinking of himself
  but the welfare of his loved ones
A single penny in his pocket
  is his blood, I can say
  is the pain and the aching bones
  is the sweat from his hard work
It is gold, a treasure
To his every step
on the pedal of his bicycle
There's a call of danger
but he ignored it all
Twenty four hours sweating,
  no sleep, no rest, no extra food

The love of a good father
Unstoppable
Unexplainable
Genuine
Unconditional
On the wheels of his bicycle
Is the dream, is his goals
That he keeps on pedaling
In a many sleepless and hungry nights
That someday
After this, no more struggles
And no more exerting too much strength
The only thing left will be
A comfortable life!

ONE FRIEND

My confidant, my counselor
A shoulder to lean on
My rock!
My Saviour!
My best friend!
You made my life complete
Lift me up when
I am falling
Holds my hands
When I feel scared
You alone can
handle my being me
You alone knows
everything about me
You guided my path
into the right tract
You never leave me
never forsake me
You love me
unconditionally
Encourages me
in times of troubles
Comforts me in times
of difficulties
My best friend
forever and ever
My GOD!

UNWANTED BOX

You are in a foreign land
away from your loved ones
Breaking your bones
from hard work
to earn a living
But also in that foreign land
All your fears happening
As you always whisper
Begging to that life threatening
pain of the unseen ailment
that eating you alive
consuming your system
can't say no to it
it's happening!
It's too early
Death snatched you
Now you're in the box
your size
Your circle mourned
Day and night
Searching for one piece
Of their broken hearts
Farewell to you sweet fellow
Unwanted box needs to rest
Rest in a place
where all
unwanted boxes laid.
May you rest in peace!
We know it's dark
Be the light
Be the bright star in the night
A guide to a lonely soul
You are there
In the night sky

From that unwanted box
You rise up
Seen in the night sky
Forever and ever
And forever
will stay
in our hearts.
Shalom!

I COME BACK STRONGER

I, I am a seed
Sown to a soil
Soil, unfertile
Soil that is dry
Soil, hard and stony.
Through the days
with seldom rain
the growth delays
The roots, slowly,
clasp the surface
to build and develop
a strong foundation.
Inside the bottle
of uncertainties,
of fear,
of stress,
of frustrations,
of struggles,
of difficulties
I, I am a seed
continue growing
in a slow motion
slowly but surely
strongly rooted.
The wind of
hazardous blow
can't move
the seed
that now
become a tree,
strong and free!

THE SCENERY

Sparkly
Like a starry night sky
Beautiful and bright
Like a forest
with a bunch of fireflies
My heart
leaps with the sight
Every night
I tend to wait
The light in darkness
keeps me calm
Brings relief,
assurance
that in every darkness
in due time
in the perfect time
You'll witness
the glamorous light
shine!
Shines through the soul.
Busy running around
for the daily errands
Streets loaded
with all kinds of transportation.
Many we don't know
they just pass by
But at the end
of the day
when the night expires
This busy street
will become lonely
and empty
Like the migrant workers
Especially domestic helpers

Alone
in the four corners
Of their employers
servants' quarters!

THE SWEET NECTAR

Struggles everywhere
Which we can't compare
Each one of us has our own journey
To deal with everyday

Each of us has goals to reach
Every steps seems hard to fetch
If your steps is unlikely working
Change your strategies and keep on moving

Nothing is impossible in this world
To a man who strive hard for a gold
Going out from the comfort zone of life
To taste the sweet nectar of success as highlight

Nectar is so sweet
Like a bee struggles flying through a monsoon air just
to taste it
So delicious, you will feel like heaven
That's the feeling when success to you is given

WINNER

Believe me
Even you're not a pro
But you're determined
You will win!

Feeling tired
But you continued fighting
Kneeling to God
You will win!

Juggling the problems
The quiz of life
You've overcome it
You're winning!

Benevolent fighter
Excellent positive mindset
Never gives up
Now you're winning!

PEACE IS MORE PRECIOUS THAN TRIUMPH

Peace
Calm, relaxed
No noise, no wars
No crimes, no victims
No poverty and homeless
Clean surroundings
Everyone in unity and
Spreading humanity.
Like a bride's gown
Pure white, no stain
At peace when happy
A joyful feeling.
At peace when you're on a hammock
Hanging between tall trees
Under the shadow of the moon
In front of the calm lake
With bonfire.
At peace when with loving friends
sharing laughter and memories
Shoulders to lean on
Always there to catch you when you fall.
At peace when you reach your goal in life
No more struggles, no more sad tears
Only smiles and laughter
Together with family you always longed for.
At peace when under the sun
Playing with the waves of the ocean
Collecting shells at the seashore
Sun bathing and reading your favorite book.

At peace when listening to your favorite music
Watching your favorite TV show
Sipping slowly your favorite coffee
Eating, savoring and enjoying your favorite food
Cuddling romantically the love of your life
Just chilling, no hatred, no enemies.

TORCH OF HOPE

Hold on unto the light
That makes life so bright
Keep the flames burning
Spread it with a heart smiling

Unique and one of a kind
Very rare to find
Generously capable
Of sharing love and beyond humble

Strong yet soft-hearted
To the surroundings is not blinded
Vigilant as never expected
And to wrong you are straightly corrected

Hold on unto the light
Give peace between a fight
Make each day worthy
Make ourselves happy.

WIN WITH SELF-DISCIPLINE

When you think of something
Don't forget to do the planning
Win it with self-discipline
Allow your efforts to be seen

If you want to be successful
Go out from your comfort zone, stroll
Work out your goal, neat and clean
Win it with self-discipline

The moment you are aiming to win
Win it with self-discipline
Don't allow procrastination
Never stop, go straight to your destination

Win your dream in life with self-discipline
Focus accordingly, you're the captain
No one else will do it for you
Make it happen, work for it, don't let go!

NATURE IS THE ANTIDOTE

Out of the sudden blow
From a feeling of deep sorrow
That nobody is there
That nobody care
Nature is the antidote

Run into the forest
From an aching soul, rest
Enjoy the beauty of nature
Hug it when feeling down and in failure
Nature is the antidote

Visit the flowers that bloom
Will light up your day from a gloom
Lonely in a faraway land
Homesickness kills from a distant bond
Nature is the antidote

Migrants miss their home
Having no choice but to bear it alone
On the beaches they donated their tears
Ocean welcomes it, calming their fears
Nature is the antidote

Truly nature heals
How happy and relaxing it feels
When nature caress you from sadness
And saved you from total madness
Thank God cause nature is an antidote.

52

SUMMIT

The crown of nature
The pride of each mountain
The peak, comfort to a stranger
The tower, on top of every fountain

Summit, beautiful and amazing
Sceneries that relaxes the eyes
A cooling effect, I can't stop on gazing
Form the summit, winners arise

A climb, a hike that is so tiring
Under the heat or the embrace of the winter wind
A journey that is so interesting
Summit is sometimes hard to reach and hard to find

In life, summit is our success
Climbing is our struggles and difficulties
But be happy and proud of the progress
You've been learning on the way, of your capabilities

Your crown
Your pride
Your pedestal
The symbol of your strength

BONUS

Any worker would wish
For an appreciation from their boss
In terms of money, to put on their table a good food

Sometimes to their unexpected loss
They need money, so bonus is a huge help
But in reality, this is only done by a few boss

Migrant workers just give a yelp
Because majority suffers from their employers
And bonuses are forgotten, employers keep them in
their shelf

Blessed are those who has a good and generous
employers
Sorry for those who have not yet
And working to a self-esteem destroyers

But with or without bonus, never forget
To work honestly and always give your best.

CRAFTED WITH HEART

Being a migrant is not easy
Flew away from dear family
Working hard to earn money
Sweat, blood, pains, homesickness
Sent their love humbly
Crafted with heart
The migrants
Heroes
Bold

Their heart aims to help their family
Sacrificing their own self-wants
To provide great convenience
Far in a foreign land
Discriminated
But still stands up
Not shaken
Thinks of
Hope

THE WARRIOR

Brave and strong
In homesickness they sing a song
They are bullied and often accused wrong
But with bravery, easy for them to get along

Migrant workers are warriors
They break all the barriers
Even in a faraway land they became worriers
But their strengths are their victories

In the midst of unexpected ugly phenomenon
While working abroad, it is common
Massive determination is out and grown
The warrior in them serves as their rainbow crown

Woe to you who underestimated them deeply
For you do not know what they've experienced
discreetly
They keep it by themselves to avoid stress
completely
And let their family back home live happily

Warriors we can't compare to anybody
Their bravery and strength exposed fully
They have this determination molded uniquely
I am a witness of their warrior shield woven neatly

Salute to all migrant workers
That in hardship perseveres.

BEYOND THE STORM

It is said, beyond the storm there's a sun
Sun that shines so bright
Brighter than glimmering stars
Stars in a clear sky at night
Night that is blank and dark
Dark but it is only temporary
Temporary because God is the true light

"I am the light" God said
Said it, telling us all not to be afraid
Afraid not from all these struggles
Struggles that created a storm
Storm that goes and travels beyond
Beyond what we can handle sometimes
But sometimes it is just a feeling because beyond the storm, our God is waiting.

DEATH VALLEY

Eagles flew
Sailed into the wind
And off they go
Into a place they don't know
Eagles settled in
Build their nests and rest
Exploring the new valley
Flowing of milk and honey
Enough of treasures to collect
A place where massive opportunities
are laid, free to take
Sometimes, eagles got overwhelmed
Crosses the line
Wasting the time
Wasting the body
Go into the death valley
Without knowing it
Already consumed with poison
And it's late
It is too late
To realize
that it is the end
Already the dead end.

TRANSFORM YOUR FUTURE

Transform your future
When you think you are behind
And success is hard to find
Move and work hard, don't remain blind

Transform your future
When you are down below and struggle
From poverty you are always in trouble
Seek a piece and complete the puzzle

Transform your future
Don't just sit at the corner and wait
And rate yourself for only an eight
Stand up and never give up, keep the faith

Transform your future
From agony and deep sorrow
Keep going and join the brighter tomorrow
Because God is there, leading, for us to follow

Transform your future to a happy one
That anyone else feels, in life's race we won.

BELIEVE IN YOUR DREAMS

Beneath the struggles of life
Eliminate all the doubts from the strife
Leave the pains of the past
Instill to the mind that it won't last
Ensure that our dreams are always intact
Venture to it following the right track
Evolve and fulfill our dreams, step by step, like every
tick of the clock

Inner peace is necessary, avoid any doubt
Never get frustrated, never quit, that's all about

You are a warrior, believe in your dream
Observe confidence, maintain your self-esteem
Understand the steps, understand the process
Remember to stay focus to avoid certain looses

Dare to dream and make it happen
Remove uncertainties, make your path clean
Emblem of our success is our strong belief of winning
Acknowledging the pros and cons, an advantage of
gaining
Mold our mind into positivity
Success is on its way, claim it, receive it, victoriously

A BLESSING IN DISGUISE

Life is worth living
It is worth risking
Life is full of failure
Step on it, don't nurture

Negative and positive outcomes
Enter the world and it welcomes
Let the bleed of your skin
Scream the sound of your win

Never hesitate to try
Keep moving, never let your oil dry
Try and try to see the error
Gain your success, scare away the terror

Please keep this in mind
Cure to failure is easy to find
To a mindset that is positive
And throws away all the negative

Failure is a blessing
A lesson worth confessing
It is a step towards success
So take the risk, don't be afraid and be blessed

STOP DELAYING

Stop delaying!

You are a worm
Soft and slow
From eating, leaves deform
Even stopping seeds to grow

Stop delaying!

You are a turtle
Hiding from your shell
Sleeping into your comfort zone, piling up hurdle

Stop delaying!

You are too lazy
Stagnant, doing nothing
Stop being unreasonable crazy

Stop delaying!

You are conceited
You think you know everything but you're not
You think you win but you're defeated

Stop delaying!

Get up my friend
Stand up from negativity
Make productive, the life that you gained

BE A CONQUEROR OF FEAR

To conquer fear
   is the beginning of wisdom
So listen carefully dear
   absorb this quote to your system

I've learned that it is
   just a superstition
Don't settle for this
   it blocks your goals and ambition

It is said to be
   the main source of cruelty
makes you blind, you can't see
   let's you speak negative, fluently

So I'm asking you to learn
   to be a conqueror of fear
let that fear to be burn
   put it into ashes, let it disappear

Let the venom of it gone
   cured by the power of bravery
Thy strong will be done
   cast the power of fear away

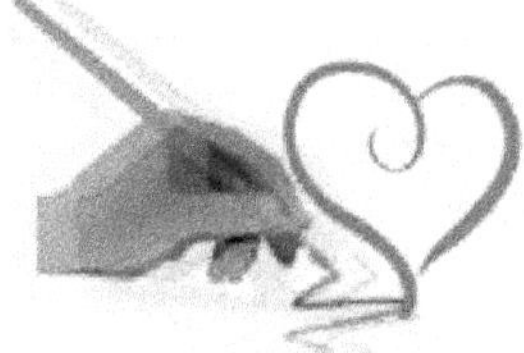

WHAT IS HAPPINESS?

I, myself don't know
If there are really rules to happiness
If there's a thread to follow
To eliminate all the sadness

I just live a simple life
Euphoria I always have
Setting my mind to forsake the strife
And instead, count my blessings with love

When I go out from my abode
I'm spreading free smile to everyone
It's contagious, that's how I showed
How I live my life and how it began

Happiness is a choice
Happiness is deep within
Let it be heard from our voice
Let it be seen from our grin

Share! Share! Share!
Give! Give! Give!
For happy is a cheerful giver
Leave an impact, a memorable life to live.

PROCRASTINATION

Hey Jude! Dude!
Sweet words
from your lips
like honey
from a nectar
collected to a honeycomb.
Words, powerful
as an explosives
but only remains
as sweet words
for it becomes rotten.
No action!
Stagnant!
Laziness in your mind
was already set
Procrastinating!
You don't move
a light post
without electricity.
Hey dude! Later!
Later, the word that came out
from your small unsmiling mouth
What a shame!
What a shame that
you let things pass
the opportunity went gone
Keep on waiting,
Waiting!
waiting!
Without working on it
Leads you to failure
Now, you cry a river
realizing, all dreams gone
Vanished!

ADDICTED TO SUCCESS

I am....addicted to success
Success is programmed to my mindset
Mindset that was nurtured by positivity
By positivity, I was able to rise
To rise from the pain of life
Life is so cruel and chaos
Chaos world that gives us pressures
Pressures, it drags us down, me and you
You might feel uncomfortable
Uncomfortable and feeling down
Down into the pit of failure
But failure is the beginning of success
Success served to those who persevere
Perseveres and don't quit
Don't quit pursuing the dreams
Dreams that was on the top
On the top to reach and realize
Realize and make it happen
Happen to those addicted to success
Success is my goal, yes it is
Yes it is, I am

BE STILL AND KNOW

Be still and know
You are a winner
You're here to deliver
The best version of you

Be still and know
You're full of courage
Having the ability to fix the damage
Let the roar of the lion resemble you

Be still and know
You're not insane
You defeated the pain
You are resilient, yes it's you

Be still and know
Despite of difficulties
There are a lot of opportunities
Open it, the key is you

Be still and know
You're not a failure
Set your goals and secure
The only driver of your life is you

THE GREAT IMPACT

We are living in this world
Without knowing what would be the future
Our minds go twirled
Got pained, broken, cut, and closes suture

The lives that go weary
Having those feelings of uneasiness
Eliminate it all with positivity
Great impact must be on top for success

Lead as an example by heart
Positive impact always has a ripple effect
Leave the past and make a new start
A good heart is a legacy that makes life perfect

If tomorrow we will die unexpectedly
Our great impact on others will live forever
Showing them to take things calmly and collectedly
Following the wisdom from above which is greater

HEAVEN ON EARTH

What a beautiful world
    it would be
If everyone is at peace
    and live happy

All were living in harmony
    without jealousy
Oh what a heavenly feeling
    it would be

Spirit of brotherhood
    oneness and camaraderie
A fulfilled parenthood
    to a child with glee

All creatures are free
    not in a cage of entertainment
Living in their habitat and community
    with love, care, and contentment

Heaven on earth, I pray
    no wars, no struggles, and pains
Everyone must be in unity
    let's revive humanity!

SHAPE YOUR MINDSET

Shape your mindset
  to think something better
    to think positivity
      to be a winner

Shape your mindset
  to ignore something that fails
    to leave behind negativity
      to overcome struggles

Shape your mindset
  to learn something new
    a new skill that will lead you
      to a better and successful future

Shape your mindset
  to stand alone strong
    in the midst of difficulties
      and be a conqueror

Shape your mindset
  in a Godly manner
    because in this world
      we alone, without God, are nothing

Shape your mindset
  to ignore arrogance
    to defeat stupidity
      but to enhance self-beauty

Shape your mindset
  that no matter what
    in sickness and in health
      you will fight life to the end

MEDIOCRITY

Once I saw you crying
At the corner, from bullying
You started to think you're not enough
That your talent is but a piece of crap

Hercules grant you with unbelievable strength
Nothing can defeat you even with tenth
Venus pass on to you her beauty
Staring at you, princes can't concentrate on their duty

So why you are confused of yourself?
You are a gem, a treasure, and a great help
Your voice is a nightingale of the night
Gives calmness and eases away all fright

Apollo gave you a seed of poetry
Even teach you in the field of archery
You are gifted enough to say,
That you're not good that much, it's a hearsay

You are diamond and a gold
Your legacy will never become old
Your advocacy is a beautiful sunray
Leaves wisdom, gives inspiration, all throughout the
days.

PRETENTIOUS ROYALS

Royal highness you want to be
With a fake crown, that's what I see
Dressed with a signature designer
Credits exploded, woe to you social climber

Witnessing your walk, you won
Table etiquette is perfectly done
But didn't have a palace of their own
Their true colors aren't shown

Living life like royals in palaces
Kings and queens, princes and princesses
They're extremely dreaming of it
Their arrogance doesn't fit

When is the time you're gonna see?
Form blindness you're going to be free?
To realize the simplicity of life counts
Not pretending so no more hurt from bounce

Showing off of money doesn't mean you're rich
And having no money doesn't mean you're poor
Perspective towards positivity is rich
Negative mindset with trillions of money is poor

Pretentious royals you are
You can't pretend that far
The stress will always drag you down
The secret you're hiding will let you drown

Consequences might steal your sanity
Pretending will lead you into vanity
The end is surely a huge fall
The bad karma is coming to start its call

UNCONTROLLED DESIRE

Heart breaker!
You adore lustful desires
Thinking only
of your own happiness!
Your deed is
a two-edged sword
that cuts each strand
of veins in the body
of the heart.
A woman
Yes, a woman
having a wounded heart
for the husband
has a lover
She is dying from hurt
deep hurt and yes it is.
You, man of uncontrolled desire
You forsake your promise
you took for granted
the woman, the wife
and from that one ounce
of a sudden pleasure
you leave your wife
dying from inside
of her bleeding soul.
A man
Yes, a man
with a muscle strong and hard
hard like a wall
but the wall collapsed
down into pieces
He was salvage
he was dead
from the pain.

You woman!
Look into another man
Devoured by uncontrolled desire
You slept with a home wrecker
In a flash of lightning and thunder
Under the rain,
a heavy rain
the moon is hiding
a witness
of a wrecked home
from what we call
uncontrolled desire.

GREAT THINGS NEVER CAME FROM A COMFORT ZONE

When you feel comfortable
It means no progress
You stop there on top of the table
Because you're already feeling at ease

Great things need to chase
Need to continue working hard
Small step is okay, don't make haste
Just don't stop, reach your card

You sleep because you think it's done
Contented of only one success
Doing so, you missed all the fun
And the lessons along each progress

Embracing the comfort zone, laziness!
Missed opportunities because you remain immobile
You thought in your comfort zone there's total
happiness
Only to find out, it creates damage and it's fatal

DETOUR

When you know that going ahead
Will cause your heart to bleed
Detour!

When your plans are not working
And your head continues aching
Detour!

When your purpose is not appreciated
And you end up standing alone and aggravated
Detour!

When you feel you are too comfortable
And delaying things, no challenges that are able
Detour!

Detour!
Because procrastination delays your success
And you need to free yourself from madness

Detour!
Make another suited plan to realize
And stick to it, make it! Finalize!

Detour!
To avoid something toxic and dangerous
For your own health, happiness, and humane
purpose

UNTWISTED MIND

You are strong
You are determined
You are courageous
You know your purpose
You are unbeatable
You are kind
You are loving
You know your worth
You are true and genuine
You are beautifully made
You are a hero
You know your plans
You are brave
You are one of a kind
You are knowledgeable
You know your goal
You are having a positive mind
You are not shaken with problems of any kind
You are an inspiration
You have a great dedication
Your mind is fixed, untwisted
Decides very carefully
You are a master of your mind
You've reached your dreams, successfully.

LISTEN TO THE SOUND OF THE SIDEWALK

Brooom.....brooo......brooom
Sound echoing, so deafening
The dawn looks gloom
My eardrums running away from exploding

I saw a masterpiece
From my sight, I can't erase
Begging for the sunrise kiss
To stay away from a drowning bliss

The sound of the sidewalk
Reaches the moon above
Asking for a romantic talk
Until the hearts melt with love

Mesmerizing it is, the sidewalk offers
The strength of mighty Hercules
I will smell, sip and taste
Inhale and savor it
Spit it out until my tongue goes dry
Try to lick it from me
And express what's like to be
My everlasting feeling, I'm proud
Offered to the sidewalk, shout it loud
The echoing sound never-ending
I will love the sound of the sidewalk, until then
It is worth defending.

I will reach for the stars
touch it, count it one by one
hold it, a fragile diamond
Let it shine, so holy and divine
Lights up the whole world
Sound heard into the entire universe.
Secure the sound, tighten the hold.

LIGHT OF GLORY

The light illuminating
It is so captivating
You will love the brightness
Brings each soul to calmness

The reflection of light
Shines unto you, so bright
Covered your soul
Lift your spirit up from a fall

The light of glory
Given to you with love and mercy
Protecting you from temptations
A shield from unseen tribulations

God above is our light
Helping us all from our fight
A fight against this cruel world
Cruelty that nowadays unfold

Light that's majestic, it is enchanting
It is a gift, I won't stop believing.

SLOW DOWN

It is very tiring, right?
Conquering the battle that we fight
In that case
Slowdown!

I know you are exhausted
Yes you are strong but you also get frustrated
The reality that we can't deny
It is a fact
So in that case
Take a break and rest
Slowdown!

It is not a crime to slow down
Have a sacred moment to eliminate the frown
To give ourselves a pure relaxation
And think twice, thrice, strengthen the determination
Grow more our inspiration
So we can start again strong
And we can share it with the community we belong
Sometimes the rush is dangerous
We can't think carefully of the cons and pros
So let us slowdown a bit
Slowdown, it's for the best
Slowdown!

BE A HOUSEFLY

Each one of us has a purpose
Each one of us has a talent
Each one of us was created unique
Each one of us is important

But as we live
Learn how to give
Use our purpose
Share it, don't curse!

Nowadays we suffered from pollution
For so many years, we don't have a solution
Plastic scattered everywhere
Mother Earth is grieving, it is unfair!

Be a housefly that loves recycling
From rotten goods, they are happy eating
Leaving the surroundings clean from dirt
Please learn to recycle, help our Mother Earth!

STIRRING UP CONFLICT

Woe to you!
You who has a twisted tongue
You who stirs up the conflict
Conflict in the community
Conflict in between family
Conflict between friends
Creating conflicts that never ends

Woe to you!
You who has an envious heart
Form evil deeds, you never depart
When are you going to stop?
When are you going to change?
Is your heart cold and frozen?
And ignored God, cut the seal of being chosen?

WISDOM CALL

To you people
God sends a call
It is a wisdom's call
So please listen
Listen with your hearts open
People who listen
Will acquire more knowledge
Foolishness will come to finish
Crooked mind will vanish
But those who don't listen
Foolishness is their gain
The fear of the Lord,
is the beginning of wisdom.

MOCKERS, FOOLS, THE SIMPLE

Mockers
A slithering snake
Has poisonous venom
Ready to bite
Killer of the fair fight
Fools
A massive flock of pretended ignorance
Thou heart was covered with great vengeance
You acted smart but end up sorry
Darkened up the God's glory
The simple
The least harmful but lazy
How long you will stay crazy?
Wicked thou art
To God's wisdom, you depart.

POOR AND HELPLESS

Riches on the floor
Golds, diamonds
treasures galore!

Everywhere is sparkling
sound of fame
heard from a welcome of bells ringing

On the pedestal, you are there
screaming your riches
but no one mind it, no one gives a care

You feel so empty and useless
longing for something to give you real happiness
realizing that fame and money is not the true riches

So poor and helpless
in the midst of riches
you are alone, seems hopeless

the true treasure of all
is a heart of gold
that answered God's call

Less fortunate are blessed
the moment they embrace the gospel
riches will be showered upon them to their request.

HINTS OF FAILURE

Devastated!
You are a walking dead
A weak body
of a paralyzed one
You sip the destruction
You nurture the addiction
Sitting at the corner
you lost your sanity
Why?
Why such a stupid deed?
Your eyes turned purple
Smoke occupied the space
Toxic and pollution
You turned into a monster
a barbarian
You consumed the failure
Surrounded you, are solutions
You become blind
You closed your heart
You shut your mind
You're lost!
Rise!
Arise, my friend,
You are strong
and not a failure
You have a purpose to fulfill
Arise!

WHERE IS THE CAMARADERIE?

Once, you were all together
Like we can tell, it will be forever

One goal, one dream, one mind
With extraordinary talents, seldom failed

With a great positive perspective
Knowledgeable and beyond creative

But one day, something went wrong
Commitment gone as if no one belongs

Poisoned with ego, everyone go
Where is the camaraderie, my fellow?

Remember each one is important
Highly appreciated, your support and advertent.

ONLY GOOD THINGS

Forget the belief
  that when we do good
    we are out from grief

Forget the idea
  that only good things will happen
    to those who are doing good deeds

Forget it! Forget it!

The truth is that
  we experienced good and bad
    it is up to us
      how to handle it
        based on our own perspective

That's why forget the belief
  the belief of a negative mind
    feed our mind with positivity
      so we can handle the pain and grief
        solutions are always there easy to find
          stand up and embrace prosperity.

THAT KIND OF BELIEF

I can see your belief
        Relief
It shines and glows
        Flow
Flows into my veins
        Reigns
The belief that spread
        Bread
I am full and was inspired by you
        Too
Your determination is so high
        Sky
And that belief flies like a dove
        Love
The rays of love shine through your skin
        Win
No matter what, I believe
        Relieve
There's success in due time
        Climb.

NURTURE YOUR GIFT

Is life difficult and painful?
    Gainful
From the experiences of day to day
    Say
Learn from struggles and pain
    Gain
The victory that is hard to find
    Mind
Self-enhancement is a must-do
    You
You are a fierce warrior
    Worrier
Nothing to worry with your strength
    Length
No matter how fast or slow you move
    Prove
The genuinity of your actions
    Factions
The group you are in, tells who you are
    Far
And near, you are one, in a desire
    Require
The most needed of all is that wit
    Grit.

THE VERDICT IS IN

Stubborn human being
following their own desire
in God's way, they keep on fleeing

Are you that kind
so stubborn and wild
lost the right path, become blind

The verdict is in, was laid
consequences of our deeds
we are accountable, but God paid

How shameful are we
ruining the paradise, made for us
to comfort us and it's free

This time the verdict is different
bad equals bad, good equals good
we know it, we are not ignorant!

ON THIS ROAD CALLED LIFE

Zigzag, crooked
As we move forward
Sometimes we reach
the dead end.
Along our way
lots of road signs
but we ignored it.
The road is uncertain
there's wide like curtain
beware of the narrow one
to get through it is not fun.
On this road called life
we might experience pain
peace that is difficult to maintain
struggles that might blow our brains.
Be happy when it is straight
walk to it with faith
this life might bring a curse
so don't live with anything false.
The road, unpredictable
as we travel
Be always ready
coz there is room
to hail a great success
and a room to fail.

BABY'S BREATH

Smells so pure
Like a cure
Smells like perfume
makes you bloom
A baby's breath
wins over death
Clean and innocent
Symbol of purity
Smells that relaxes
brings inner beauty
mind into clarity.
I am fascinated
without a doubt
the baby's breath
is a symbol of cleanliness
and peace.
Should we let it remain
in our hearts and surroundings?
Yes!
A flower, white
Charming and the innocence
are sincerity and love
a compassion and trust
A romance.

TEAMWORK

The most important asset in a team

Emerging attitude that gives a gleam

Acquiring through practice and self-discipline

Making the group strong for a win

Working for it everyday without ceasing

Offering love to everyone who's participating

Real camaraderie grows within

Keeping the bond of teamwork is a great gain.

THE SECRET GARDEN

Alone in the place where no one knows
There, a secret garden that glows
Home for all creatures great and small
Surrounded by trees that grow so tall

A fairy named Angelina is the owner
A fairy with a good heart, so dear
Her garden is a treasure out from her love
All creatures are happy with a home they have

Oh! what a beautiful place
Full of abundance and grace
Wish I can live there for once
Savoring the beautiful scenery in a glance

The secret garden that brings peace and joy
To the greedy ones, they tried to destroy
But a good heart defeated it with might
Because God completed it with a good fight.

SANCTUARY

The pain trembles
and fear arise
like an angry lightning
to the sound of thunder.
Misfortune greeting
like Anaconda's mouth
slithering and ready to devour.
Toasted under the heat
of scorching sun
The hell of agony
needs to vanish forever.
Scavengers crowded
the vast universe
of richness and abundance
felt the full force punch
into their rumbling stomach.
HUNGER!
Are you having a heart of stone?
Are you blind?
You see but you ignore,
passing through them
chin up, standing tall.
Would you like to offer
something humane?
If I may,
I would like a sanctuary.
HOMELESS!
let them
curl up their body
feeling comfy, cuddling comfort
out from a world
of too much chaos
too much pain
too much fear

too much misfortune
And why?
Co'z of humongous crocodile around
always ready to bite
with their long sharp pangs,
the small prey.
I wish I can help
in my small act of kindness
to preserve humanity
in my dream of
Godly sanctuary
to those who deserve
and worth it
to savor it freely.
So help me God!

SAFE HAVEN

You know when I was young
We lived in a loafing shed
And into my parents' arms, I clung

Then my father was gun shotted
I've been told because of jealousy
So that time, at night, we fled

Out of curiosity
I'm looking for an answer
Why we are treated so poorly?

From that moment on, I made a planner
I wrote all my goals in life
Including a house for the family, even newcomer

Despite hardships and strife
I am proud that I surpassed it all
But the struggles are like a deep cut of a knife

I dreamed of a house with a huge and wide hall
To welcome everyone who needs comfort
To serve as a safe haven for all

A house with ambiance of love, not hurt
Surrounded by fruit trees, vegetables and flowers
Backyard with my favorite dart

With fountain that showers
A modern classic design
And cozy chambers

I love cooking, so kitchen is mine
Modular it will be and all painted white

Everyone is welcome to eat, and it's fine

This house will serve as a light
For those who go astray and starve
To continue life and fight

A shelter that makes people a well carve
Carved with strength and positivity
And to God they serve

Simple house full of possibilities
The place that will serve as training center
For the young generation to show their capabilities

Capability to reach their goal and enter
Enter to a safe haven and go out with pride
Proud that they will also succeed, who knows? maybe
an inventor

Molded life with strength from its low and high tide
They were rescued, brought to a safe haven where
human angels reside.

I LOVE YOU
Written by: Juliette Ogier

When I see you
I love you
When we make cookies
I love you
When we are fighting
I still love you
When I read with you
You make me so happy
But when I'm not with you
I'm bored
So I ask my parents
Can I invite my friends?
Please?
Like, I love them too.

WHO AM I?

To those who want to know me better
Listen carefully including my hater
I am simple, not that perfect
To my loved ones, I'm ready to protect

I do sometimes forget
But of course, I don't regret
Because it gives me lessons
To mind things that lead to progressions

I'm not perfect at my work
But I do it with a heart, I'm not a jerk
I am a human with a positive mindset
All my goals are having time set

I am resilient, don't dare me
I am bold, I was born to be
You don't treat me, right?
I can give you a good smile and not a fight

I was born with positivity
I don't give up easily, I've learned things
cooperatively
I've worked with people, developed loyalty
To my superior, my respect is a royalty

I am simple and always happy
Many problems, I prayed to God verbally
I am a conqueror of fear
To all hindrances of success, I'm ready to tear

I am a domestic helper, working for so many years
I am proud of it, I am a person with a heart that cares
Most of all who am I? I am me
Never change me the way you wanted me to be!

GREAT PRETENDER

Your smile
when you see me
is sweet like honey
You talked to me
like an angel
You seemed so perfect
so good to be true
but you had a poison
Stabbing me at my back
behind my knowledge
but God is so good
never allows you
to ruin my being.
You keep on complaining
you slithering snake
with a poisonous venom
pretending to be a sheep
meek and very quiet
But you secretly
spreading the venom.
You are weak!
You cannot confront me
instead, you took someone
then complain of
another person, of me
Perfect!
Perfection!
Perfectionist!
Great pretender!
Wake up!
Wake up from a negative thought
Pretending to be nice
Is your heart still pumping?
You are decaying

Useless are those nice words
Useless are those sweet smiles
Useless!
Useless!
I hope you'll get the courage
to be true to yourself
So you can show it to others
The true genuine kindness!
You are silent
You played safe
Yet you are........
A great pretender!

A HELPER, A HUMAN, NOT A SLAVE

Hired as a helper
Treated as a slave
Not all, but majority of the employer
Stole helper's freedom, leaving them to bereave

Working long hours without consideration
Bosses around, don't want to see helper's sitting
down
This is a sad truth upon migration
Admit it or not, rest hour, to employer is a frown

This is based to a true to life stories
Of migrant workers across the whole world
Discrimination, racism, division, are they full of
riches?
Helpers are humans but humanity has been curled

It is true that you paid them a salary
But bear in mind, they worked hard and ached their
bones
During a day off, some still work and it seems ad
turned out to be compulsory
Even disrespect their freedom with high harsh tones

Or sometimes playing a guessing game
Unpredictable attitude of employers is a pain
It creates stress, oh what a shame!
Lack of good communication has no gain

Lack of sleep from long hours of duty
Waking up at 5 AM, working 'till midnight
With dark circles, their eyes lost its beauty
15 to 18 hours duty a day, helpers health slowly out
of sight

Please be reminded of this one rule
Don't do to others what you don't want others to do
to you
It's also you're choice to remain as a fool
But consequences, karma, will definitely hunt you

Kudos to all good employers and workers!

ODE TO MY FAMILY
by: Juliette Ogier

My dad is quite funny
Swimming is his hobby
He loves bicycling and hiking
Oh! and he also loves eating
My dad is good, loving, and kind
He is always in my heart and my mind.
My mom is the best mom in the whole world
She is beautiful
She loves to see us happy
She takes us to water world,
Ryze Hongkong and restaurants
Verm city and buying us new clothes.
Maxime is my older brother
He loves to annoy us when he gets bored
Maxime loves to read books
He worries when there are lightnings
But I love him so much!
Arthur is my little brother
He loves playing with toy cars,
airplanes and trucks
He pulls our hair and I don't know why?
I love my family so much!

COVID-19
by: Juliette Ogier

When covid-19 came
it was not fun
You know why?
Because we are stock
home school
home office
parks are closed
beaches are closed
We can't play outside freely
There is quarantine when you travel
3 weeks quarantine
You can't even open your windows
We have to wear a mask
You have to make one meter
social distancing
of only two people
then four people
If you want that the virus goes away
you have to be vaccinated
I hope that everybody is safe
and make sure to not
have the virus
I am so sad.......
we can't go home yet to Switzerland.

HONEY BUNNIES
by: Juliette Ogier

I have a bunny
her name is Oreo
she is black and white
she is 6 months and a half old
she loves when we pet her
but she does not like
when we stare at her, eating
when she sleeps, she makes sure
that Cookie is not beside her.
I have a bunny
her name is Cookie
she has lots of different browns,
brown fur on her
she is 5 and a half old
she loves running around
on our roof top
she is very aggressive sometimes
when she is scared
but if you hold her slowly
and you stay calm
she can be calm too.
One last thing, I can tell you
that I love them
soooooo much!

BEWARE, BE AWARE, BE REAL

Beware!
Not all people clapping
are happy of your success
of your achievements
of your fame!
Be vigilant enough
to know the difference
of toxic and genuine
We are living in a world
where competition
has reached its evil deal
Beware!
Be Aware!
Be aware, that you're not the only one
who need care
who needs love
People need understanding
Be aware of your surrounding
give your best in sharing
Open your heart, mind
soul and eyes
don't be blind
Arise and be proud, proclaiming
that God made you
a channel of His blessing.
Be Real
Stand up in the middle of the unreal
get rid of the fake
and continue being real
genuine
gold
precious jewel
thank you for being real.

OASIS

Oasis
Yes, you are!
A shoulder to lean on
A listener we can count on
A hope!
Our only hope
Covid-19 came,
a theft of happiness
and freedom
of all human being
God is the oasis
The only one
where water found
relieve our thirst
People were fed up
of this covid protocols
We are living in a world
that is slowly dying
slowly come to an end.
When this pandemic end?
The world economy
dries out.
Struggles and pains
Children are stressed
in their young age
experiencing all this!
Where is freedom?
Where is the place
that we call paradise?
But thank God!

still, we found
an oasis
in a desert of pains.
Keep strong!
Stay safe!
Keep the faith!

DANGER ZONE

You are evil
You took away the calmness
the sweet embrace, of a soft
curling waves of
oceans that cleanse
all the worries and anxieties
Look at the surrounding?
You turned it hell, scorching
Birds flew in a haste
Paradise became a waste
Oh danger zone, be gone!
You are wicked, you are rotten
Your flaming anger was stirred up
Why are you so scrofulous?
You imprisoned the beauty
of the greenery, of paradise
turned it to a bloody torture
no feeling of ecstasy.

FAMILY IS LOVE

The core foundation of love
A home blessed with God above
A place where a lot of experiences to share
Called a family with love and care

A family that prays together
Also believed to stay forever
No matter what struggles they encounter
A family hold on tight to each other

Even in the deepest sorrow, they are one
Supporting one another, having a strong bond
In sickness and in health, there is unity
Togetherness with each responsibility

Family love is pure and unconditional
Family that creates a home of freedom, is an
additional
The core of building a character
The core of building a character, ready to face their
life's chapter.

THE REMAINS

Are you not tired?
Are you not scared?
Wars, deaths, famine
Look what is the remains
This act makes my heart grieving
People scattered and starving
Victims having no shelter
Oh God! they also need water
I'm totally agitated
What's happening today is not accepted
To humanity, it is a shame
To greediness of power, it is to blame
Oh! wonderful creation
Ruined and loss of a nation
Kingdoms and palaces
Look now! was turned into ashes
Bombs and missiles
Please stay calm!
Guns and bullets
Please behave!
Be united and say no
Say no to wars that destroy
Destroy the lives of innocent people
People that only want peace
Peaceful life and with at ease
War no more
Bring back honor
So that humanity will be restored.

RIDING IN TANDEM

Back a few years ago
In the Philippines where I grew
Riding in tandem is a no, no
It creates a problem, I don't know

Either hold up or murder
Snatching items from the owner
Government view it as a big deal
Riders in tandem are so cruel

This issue creates chaos
Huge syndicates growing famous
Citizens that are victims
Mostly are not given justice as fair claims

Why does this is all happen?
To my beloved country Philippines?
Maybe because of poverty
People were dragged to be greedy.

LIFE OF A TRUCKER

Night and day, whenever, wherever
The big rig proudly deliver
Urgent needs of whoever
Sent by a strong driver
Never surrender
The fast runner
Best trucker
No fear
Dear

On the road any time of the day
Driving a truck so huge and free
Even a storm can not delay
Life of a trucker
In everyday
You are loved
Our dear
Hero

*Dedicated to Richard Bryant and to all drivers,
truckers around the world who earned a living
through driving!
GOD BLESS YOU ALL!*

SURVIVOR

You crushed me
You destroyed my inner peace
You are there
hiding in my two little breasts
Days of agony
Thinking of what it would be
Is it safe?
Is it dangerous?
You are a tiny killer
Of my sleepless nights
Of my busy days
I overthink!
Is this my end?
What about the welfare of my family?
My loved ones?
Out of this questions
I found myself in a room
White and all white
My breasts are pressed down
Checked very carefully
S-U-R-G-E-R-Y, surgery!
The word flew into the air
My eardrum seems like to explode
My heart beats so fast
Broken with the word
the deafening word
Surgery!
My days way back then
five years ago,
is a total mess
Out of this sickness
that pops up unexpectedly.
Refusing the process
of cutting off my skin with a blade,

I tried a huge total detox
Sacrificing carbs, sweets
and all unhealthy vittles.
After one year
of sincere and genuine
self-discipline
You are gone!
You are totally gone!
But you awaken
my enthusiasm
to love myself more
to value my health more.
I manage to defeat you
You poisonous lump
Yes! I am free
And I am so happy
I am free
from the bondage of fear
I survived
I am a SURVIVOR!

AGING

Are you afraid to become old?
That your skin become sag?
Sag and your face will have wrinkles?

Are you afraid to become old?
While looking at the mirror
Seeing the difference of yesterday, your today, and
your future?

Are you afraid to become old?
That you will become dependent
Dependent on someone to help you?

Are you afraid to become old?
That you're physically deteriorating
Deteriorating also mentally and becoming forgetful?

Are you afraid to become old?
Incapable of traveling alone
Afraid of some serious old age health complications?

Aging is all in the mind, they say
Go out, be active physically, and play
Relax and do it slowly

There's a lot of activities that fit elders
Exercise and be happy, don't be like worriers
You are lucky enough to reach an old age
Because some, don't enjoy it, they vanished so early.

WHERE IS YOUR HAPPY PLACE?

Where is your happy place?
Is it in the arms of your love?
Is it in the mountain summit?
Is it on the seashore?

Where is your happy place?
Ask yourself now
Is it in the church?
Is it in the school?

Where is your happy place?
Think of it now
Is it in your home?
Is it on the beach?

If you ask me
Where is my happy place
It is my heart
Where God resides

Every day in our lives
Give ourselves a break
Meditate and give ourselves alone time
To nourish our soul and reconnect with God

A happy place is where we felt happiness
The joy, calmness, and relaxed
Away from the stress that triggers toxicity
Away from a theft that stole our solemnity.

IF I COULD ONLY

If I could only turn back the time
I will not let you harm me
I will not let you hurt me
I will not let you betray me

If I could only turn back the time
I'd preferred not to know you
I'd preferred to be alone in life
I'd preferred to be happy and not cry

But how can I turn back the time?
It was already gone
My experiences don't have a hint of fun
Like an ugly duckling struggling to be a beautiful
swan

But those time that passes by
Gone with the wind, and I keep asking why?
Why I struggled a lot with the past
And now I came to realize, struggles didn't last

I've learned to accept the reality
Through time I become strong with too much
positivity, I can say
Why I've been through all this?
Because God prepared me to fulfill my duties.

SAILOR'S MOON
(dedicated to all seafarers)

In the calmness of the sea
Sailor's anxiousness flee
Relaxing from the moon's embrace
Placidity that nothing can replace

The beauty of full moon
Like a song in perfect tune
A lullaby to a sailor's ear
It vanishes his fear

Sometimes the waves go angry
Co'z daily weather vary
And sailing is not that easy
The vast ocean became creepy

Oh, God! All creations protector
Please always be with the sailor
And put the ocean into tranquility
To savor the full moon's humility.

THE ONLY ROSE

I am the only rose among the thorns
Can't be defeated by a devil with horns

Standing out beautifully brave
From toxicity, I'm proud that I'm saved

This life is so tricky
But my faith never been shaky

I stand tall and upright
Looking up to the sun and moon that shines so bright

I am the light to my family
Because that's God's purpose for me to obey
completely

God bless me to bless others
Enjoy the journey that this life offers

I wish, hope, and pray I can live a hundredfold
Keeping the fragrance of rose that was untold

To continue enjoying this life and bloom
And pull out people from their gloom.

BEING ALONE

Being alone is not a big deal
Choosing it is sometimes so relaxing, for real
Being alone is better than with toxic people around
Peaceful and quiet, a perfect calming sound

It is a perfect time to meditate
And exercise the spirit of our faith
Many can't handle being alone
Because some possess being sociable, it was known

If you ask me, which one I would prefer?
I will choose being alone sometimes but it doesn't
differ
I'm trying to balance everything
Time for myself, my alone time, and time for my
circle's meeting.

BRAVE SOUL

Long time ago, a baby girl was born
Born in the '70s where gadgets are still unknown.
Clinging to her mother's arm where comfort grown
And to her father's lullaby, she's a princess with a crown.

Time passes by, she's learning how to crawl
Her first words bring warmth to the family like a shawl.
And so forth she began to stand up alone
Walking by herself, not afraid to fall down.

Leaving the childhood days is more interesting
For she encountered different levels of living
Here comes the adolescence stage full of daydreaming
For in the mind is the love as if always there waiting.

Grand is adulthood for it is full of bad and good
Flew from her birthplace to earn and bring to the table good food.
From growing up less fortunate for her is not a hindrance
Striving hard with a positive mind, she is now in great abundance.

And when she tried her luck overseas
In the midst of huge tall buildings seems like a wilderness.
Devoured with different cultures, shocked her confidence
But what a brave soul, she is always in God's presence.

127

Pursuing her dreams is not that easy
She often dealt with unseen jealousy
Surrounded with monsters of envy
But she surpasses it all with unbelievable bravery.

The world threw her disappointments
Failures and heartaches even bad sentiments.
People used her and leaving her brokenhearted
But she never thinks revenge nor even hatred.

She existed, showered with positivity
Learning that life is chaos completely.
Never gives up even the future has no clarity
Believing that God has given her a purpose to spread
love, peace, and humanity.

She knows her game and played it confidently
Ignoring toxic surroundings, situations, emotions,
mindsets, fully.
She walks her talk and stands firm, nothing can
destroy
That's her legacy, you can have it and enjoy.

Oh, God! So loving, kind, and merciful
Granting her a one-of-a-kind brave soul.
In the midst of trials, agonies, and miseries
She is like a phoenix, burned, renewed, and rose from
the ashes.

PICNIC DAY
by: Juliette Ogier

Every Friday is our picnic day
together with our friends
We do picnic at the beach
or at the park
or to our friends house
we will bring our food
dinner
swim suit
beach bag
plates
water
glass
Our foods that our auntie prepare are
sandwiches
pasta with chicken
burger
mini pizza
tomatoes
carrots
cucumbers
yoghurt
fruits
cookies
Me and my brothers and friends love picnic!
after picnic, we do a movie night
with popcorn and marshmallows.

ABOUT THE AUTHOR

Bernadith Bueno De La Cruz, born on September 28,1979 is a native of Purok 1, Brgy. Santiago, Barotac Viejo, Iloilo. Graduated her Bachelor's degree in NIPSC-BVC Barotac Viejo, Iloilo last March 2001. She is currently working in Hongkong with the Swiss family. A member of various poetry platforms and engaged into a lot of outdoor activities like hiking and many more.

Juliette Ogier, is an eight year old girl born April 25, 2013 in Geneva, Switzerland. She lives in Singapore before and currently living in Hongkong with her family. She loves to write, painting, swimming, yoga, sailing ang many more. A very energetic kid with lots of passion.